Upcycling

3rd Edition

31 Crafts to Decorate your Living Space & Refresh your Home

by Kitty Moore

Copyright © 2017 By Kitty Moore
All rights reserved. No part of this book may be reproduced in any form without permission in writing from the author. No part of this publication may be reproduced or transmitted in any form or by any means, mechanic, electronic, photocopying, recording, by any storage or retrieval system, or transmitted by email without the permission in writing from the author and publisher.
For information regarding permissions write to author at kitty@artscraftsandmore.com.
Reviewers may quote brief passages in review.

Please note that credit for the images used in this book go to the respective owners. You can view this at: ArtsCraftsAndMore.com/image-list

Kitty Moore
ArtsCraftsAndMore.com

Table of Contents

Introduction ___ *5*
1. Painting Upholstered Furniture ___ *6*
2. Line Cupboards/Drawers with Wallpaper ___ *8*
3. No Sew Window Shades ___ *10*
4. Garden Rake Wine Glass Holder ___ *12*
5. Painted Drinking Glasses ___ *14*
6. Balloon Lace Chandelier ___ *17*
7. Window Frame Jewellery Organizer ___ *19*
8. Soda Bottle Walkway Lights ___ *22*
9. A Funky Frame for Lots of Pictures ___ *24*
10. A Frame for Frames of Photos ___ *26*
11. Quick and Easy Photo Ladder ___ *28*
12. Flower Lights to Brighten Darkest Corner ___ *30*
13. Custom Art Canvas ___ *32*
14. Mini Corkboards ___ *34*
15. Magical Magnet Board ___ *36*
16. A 'Grate' Earring Holder ___ *39*
17. Recycled T-Shirt Doormat ___ *40*
18. Always Open Hanging Laundry Bag ___ *42*
19. Gold Brick Bookends with Lace Trim ___ *44*
20. Box Tidy Chargers ___ *46*
21. Colorful Cork Mobiles ___ *48*
22. Clothesline Picture Gallery ___ *50*
23. Old Belts Become Easy Shelving ___ *52*
24. Bedroom to Boudoir ___ *55*

25. Kitchen Cool	57
26. Fresh Air Door Stops	59
27. Super Shelves for Your Bathroom	61
28. Stunningly Simple Sofa Table	63
29. Dress Your Sink to Beautify Your Bathroom	65
30. 5 Minute Bathroom Storage Solution	67
31. Trendy Yarn Lampshade	69
Conclusion	71
Final Words	73
Disclaimer	74

Introduction

All it takes is a little imagination and inspiration to refresh your home with these 31 simple and budget-friendly DIY crafts to decorate your living space!

This guide is full of ideas, tips and instructions to show how you can create both functional and beautiful transformations throughout your home.

From quick, easy and highly effective storage and shelving solutions to stunningly simple furniture ideas, here you have all the know-how to reinvigorate your home from top-to-bottom, floor-to-ceiling and all the spaces and rooms in-between.

All the materials and tools you need to complete each craft are listed along with concise, to the point instructions detailing exactly what you need to do, when and how.

1. Painting Upholstered Furniture

Materials

- Upholstered chair
- Detergent
- Chalk paint
- Paint brushes
- Sand paper
- Wood paint/varnish
- Soft wax (sealant) and brush
- Rag

Instructions

1. Clean your chair - give the cushions, legs, and arms a good scrub to make sure it's ready for the transformation. (If you need to replace the seat sponge, do so now.)

2. Start painting! Thin the chalk paint with a little water and start covering the fabric. You may need several coats, especially if there are any stains.

3. If you are painting the chair's wooden legs, sand them lightly first and apply either varnish or wood paint.

4. When the chalk painted upholstery has dried use the soft wax with a brush to seal it. Simply paint on a thick coat of wax and make sure it soaks into the paint and gets into all of the crevices.

5. Now use your clean rag to wipe off ALL of the excess wax, pressing hard into the fabric to make sure the wax is absorbed.

6. Leave the chair to 'rest' overnight and then buff with the rag to get a beautiful shiny finish or use sandpaper for a softer, to get a more distressed result.

2. Line Cupboards/Drawers with Wallpaper

Materials

- Detergent

- Tape measure, pen, and paper

- Scissors

- Wallpaper

- Double-backed-sticky tape

Instructions

1. Decide how much of the cupboards and drawers you want to cover and how high you want the sides of the paper to reach. Measure the interior space and write down the dimensions.

2. Cut the wallpaper to size, ensuring you have enough to cover the space. Fold the wallpaper tight to the sides of the drawer/cupboard.

3. Put the folded paper inside the space and fold it again to fit the depth of the space, allowing the paper to rise up the side(s) of the cupboard/drawer.

4. Take the paper out and make one straight cut with the scissors in each of the four corners along the crease of the fold.

5. Place small bits of double-backed-sticky tape in the corners of the cupboard/drawer and along the edges of the wallpaper before pressing the liner into place.

3. No Sew Window Shades

Materials

- Fabric
- Tape measure, pen, and paper
- Scissors
- Fabric glue
- Tension rods

Instructions

1. Measure your windows and cut the fabric to size, and leave an extra inch on either side and make it twice the length you require.

2. Use the extra inch on the sides to create a nice hem by simply folding the fabric and fastening it with fabric glue.

3. Fold the length of fabric in the middle, make sure you have the right side facing out, and glue the ends together to make a long loop. Slip the loop over the existing curtain pole so that it is in place.

4. Next, take a tension rod and insert it across the top of the window frame and use two or more other rods below.

5. To create the faux Roman Blind look all you need to do is insert a tension rod across the top of the window frame and add a couple more rods below it. Then fold the fabric up and over the rods until you get the perfect look. Because the rods are so easy to move, you can adjust the light levels according to your preference by moving them up and down.

4. Garden Rake Wine Glass Holder

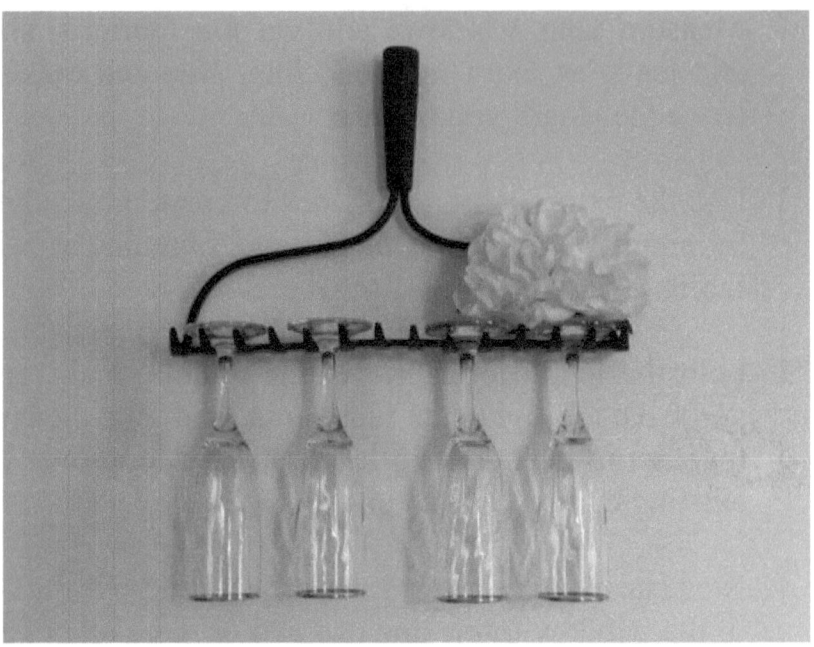

Materials

- Old metal garden rake (with blunt, curved tips)
- Detergent and scrubbing brush
- Metal spray paint (optional)
- Screw driver, drill, and wall fixings

Instructions

1. First you have to separate the rake's head from the shaft.

2. Give the metal head a good wash and decide if you want to paint it. If so, use metal spray paint to apply a couple of coats.

3. Choose where you want to hang it, and use appropriate fixings to secure the head of the rake to the wall - prongs facing outwards of course, for you to slide your wine glasses onto.

5. Painted Drinking Glasses

Materials

- Drinking glasses
- Paint brushes
- Glass paint
- Stencils and tape (optional)
- Oven and baking sheet

Instructions

1. Make sure your glasses are clean and dry before you start. If you are using stencils or a printed design stick it inside the glass with some tape.

2. Choose your colors and just paint on your design. You may want to build up layers to get stronger colors so be patient and wait for each coat to dry. When you have finished painting, remove the stencils and place the glasses on a baking sheet, and put them in a cold oven.

3. Turn the oven up to 350 degrees or its maximum heat, and leave the glasses in there for 30 minutes. Let the glasses cool before taking them out - they're now dishwasher safe and ready for use!

I have included a bonus just for you…

FOR A LIMITED TIME ONLY – Get my best-selling book "DIY Crafts: The 100 Most Popular Crafts & Projects That Make Your Life Easier" absolutely FREE!

Readers who have downloaded the bonus book as well have seen the greatest changes in their crafting abilities and have expanded their repertoire of crafts – so it is *highly recommended* to get this bonus book today!

Get your free copy at:

ArtsCraftsAndMore.com/Bonus

6. Balloon Lace Chandelier

Materials

- Inflated balloon

- Lace doilies (enough to cover the balloon)

- Wallpaper adhesive

- Paint brush

- Newspaper

- String to hang the balloon

- Scissors

- Cord to hang the chandelier

Instructions

1. Mix the wallpaper adhesive and spread out the newspaper on a table.

2. Paint the lace doily with plenty of glue so they are wet through.

3. Use the string to hang the inflated balloon and cover it with the doilies quickly.

4. Make sure the doilies overlap and paint with another layer of glue.

5. Leave the wallpaper paste covered doilies hanging until the lace is dry, possibly overnight.

6. When completely dry, pop the balloon.

7. Use the scissors to snip an opening at the top for the bulb to pass through.

8. Attach the cord to the top of the lace chandelier and hang over your light fitting.

7. Window Frame Jewellery Organizer

Materials

- Old wooden window frame
- Sand paper
- Varnish/paint
- Paint brushes
- Metal window screening
- Skinny craft wood strips
- Fabric and foam mounting boards

- Glue

- Craft knife and measuring tools

- Scissors

- Hot glue

- Hammer and small tack nails

- Screw-in hooks

Instructions

1. Clean and ready your window frame - sand, paint and varnish according to your taste and wishes. Be very careful if you have to remove the glass and metal holders, and be aware that older frames may contain lead paint so be careful when refinishing them.

2. Choose your colors and paint the frame. Allow to dry. Plan where you want your jewelry to hang by putting the frame on the floor and experimenting. Measure and cut your foam mounting boards to fit the panels. Next, cut the fabric you want to cover the boards and glue it into place.

3. Cut the metal window screening for each panel with scissors, leaving about an inch overlap on each side. Fold the sides and put the screen into place, being careful to avoid cutting yourself, and make sure it is placed at the back of the frame. Next, cut the skinny

craft wood strips to the size of the panel and place them around the window screening's four edges.

4. Lift the wood strip and screen away from the edge and run a line of hot glue around the edge of the frame and panel before pushing the wood and screen firmly back into place. Reinforce the bond when the glue has dried by hammering tiny tack nails to secure the strips and screen, making sure it is held firmly in place.

5. Fold over any overlaps of the metal screen - and be careful with splinters and cuts. Use the hot glue to secure your fabric-covered foam panels in place on the metal screen and allow them to dry. Choose where you want your hooks to hang and screw them into place around the frame. Use pins on the foam boards for lighter pieces of jewelry.

8. Soda Bottle Walkway Lights

Materials

- Empty soda bottles
- Craft knife
- Scissors
- Nail polish remover
- Painters tape
- Wire
- Dowels
- Sand (optional)
- Spray paint (optional)

- Battery powered 'candles' or LEDs

Instructions

1. Clean the bottle, removing the label and plastic ring - the nail polish remover will clean any text printed directly on the bottle.

2. Use the painter's tape to create a band around the bottle and cut a nice straight line with the craft knife.

3. Insert a dowel into the bottle top and twist the wire tightly around it. You can wrap only the mouth of the bottle or all the way up depending on your preference.

4. If you wish to spray paint the dowel and wire a particular color, now is the time. Mask off the bottle using painter's tape and newspaper. Spray on a few light coats of paint and wait to dry.

5. Put the battery operated 'candles' or LED lights into the holders. You can now create a lighted walkway to your house simply by pushing the dowels into the ground at a good height.

9. A Funky Frame for Lots of Pictures

Materials

- Old wooden frame
- Sand paper
- Varnish/paint
- Paint brushes
- Jute cording
- Hammer and small nail

- Metal screw eyes and pliers

Instructions

1. Choose your frame - any old wooden picture or window frame will do. Clean it, sand it down, and paint or distress the frame to get the look you want.

2. When dry, lean the frame against a wall with the backside facing you and use the hammer and nail to tap pilot holes at random intervals into both sides of the frame.

3. Use these holes to twist in the screw eyes - use the pliers to make it easier. Thread the jute cord through the holes from top to bottom, creating a zigzag pattern and tie it off with a strong knot at the last eye.

4. Working backwards from the bottom eye, pull the cord gently to tighten it between each eye and when you get to the top, tie that off too with a secure knot.

5. Use clothes pins/pegs or clips to attach the pictures you want to display in your new funky frame. You can now attach the frame to a wall or leave it resting on another piece of furniture and refresh your display any time you wish using the clips.

10. A Frame for Frames of Photos

Materials

- Old wooden window frame
- Sand paper
- Varnish/paint
- Paint brushes
- Jute cording
- Hammer and small nail
- Metal screw eyes and pliers

- Ribbon ties

Instructions

1. Clean and prepare the old wooden window frame according to your wants - remove all the glass (carefully!) and paint, varnish or use sandpaper to get a distressed look.

2. Select the framed photos you want to use and place them in the panels to make sure they fit. Use the hammer and nail to make pilot holes in the edges of frame where your framed photos will hang from.

3. Fix the screw eyes in place using the pliers if necessary and tie a length of jute cording from each eyelet.

4. Now tie the cord to the back of your photo frame and tie another strong knot when you are happy with the positioning.

5. Finally, use the ribbons to tie over the frame and hide the screw eyes and cord from view.

11. Quick and Easy Photo Ladder

Materials

- Branches

- Cord, ribbon, or wire for hanging

- Hammer and small nail

- Metal screw eyes and pliers

- Drill and screws

Instructions

1. This is all about the branches so try and get some nice long and straight cuts. Clean the branches and make sure they are long enough for your needs - you're making a ladder so you will need two side lengths and several cross bars.

2. Cut the branches to the desired length for the sides and the rungs. It's better if you already know what photos you want to hang so you can make sure your ladder is wide enough and that the rungs have enough space between them to fit the photos.

3. Drill holes in the side of the branches and use screws to attach the rungs (hammer and nails will also work but will not be as secure).

4. Now you have the ladder built; remember it is purely decorative so no climbing! it's time to use the hammer and nail to tap pilot holes for the screw eyes.

5. Put one on each side of the rung to secure your photos with, as they will be hanging on the leaning ladder. Decide how the frames will be held in place - either cord, ribbon, or wire - and tie that through the screw eyes, knotting it tightly. Secure the cord/wire/ribbon securely to the back of your photo frame and then tie it tightly to the screw eye below. Repeat for each photo-frame.

12. Flower Lights to Brighten Darkest Corner

Materials

- Christmas tree lights or string of LEDs
- Scissors
- Colorful cupcake liners
- Tape

Instructions

1. Gather your cupcake liners and make sure you have enough to cover all the bulbs on your string of Christmas lights, or LEDs. Use the scissors to cut the cupcake liners into flower and leaf shapes.

2. Cut a small hole into the center of each and thread the light bulb through. Attach them securely using a small piece of tape.

3. Tap a couple of nails into the wall and hang your string of colorful flower lights - turn on, stand back and bask in the beautiful glowing light.

13. Custom Art Canvas

Materials

- Artist canvas
- Gel medium (eg. Liquitex)
- Brush
- Furniture polish, oil, and cloth
- Photo-copy of your photo
- Sponge and water

Instructions

1. First you need a canvas that will fit your photo. Choose a small canvas to start and make a copy or

print out of your photo. Remember, it will be mirrored on the canvas so you might want to make adjustments if there is text, or if you want to keep the same composition.

2. Cover the canvas with a smooth, thin layer of gel medium. Place the photo image side down on the canvas. Smooth out any bubbles and make sure the whole image is sticking securely to the canvas. Leave it to dry, possibly overnight.

3. Use the sponge to gently soak the paper and once it has, begin to slowly rub off the paper, taking care not to rub away the ink. When the paper is removed you might want to 'roughen up' the edges and give the canvas a more 'arty aesthetic' which you can do by extra rubbing with a rough sponge. Allow the canvas and image to dry.

4. You will notice there is a cloudy look to the photo. Some people like this, others prefer a sharper image. If you're the latter the easiest way to achieve this is by using furniture polish or linseed oil.

5. Pour some oil onto the cloth and rub it into the canvas and notice how the image sharpens and colors deepen. That's it. All you need to do now is decide where to hang your canvas!

14. Mini Corkboards

Materials

- Coasters for cups and mugs
- Corkboard
- Brushes and paint
- Scissors, pencil, and paper
- Glue
- Drill and screws

Instructions

1. Measure the coaster and draw around its edge with a pencil onto a sheet of paper.

2. Cut a slightly smaller circle. This will be the template for cutting the corkboard to size and shape.

3. Use the circle to cut enough shapes from the corkboard. Paint your coasters in the colors you want to use. Think about where they will be going and what colors will match what you already have.

4. When they are dry, drill a hole in the center of each and then screw them onto the wall.

5. Take the corkboard circles you have cut and glue them in place. Wait for the glue to dry then start pinning up your notes, photos, ideas, and lists.

15. Magical Magnet Board

Materials

- Magnets
- Fabric or wallpaper
- Spray adhesive
- Metal baking tray
- Glue
- Foam tape
- Cord (for hanging)
- Nail and hammer

Instructions

1. You can buy small circular magnets at craft stores and decorate them yourself by gluing buttons, stickers, or bits of fabric onto them.

2. Put your metal baking tray on your fabric or wallpaper and cut around it, leaving about an inch around all sides.

3. Stick strips of foam tape along the edges of the back of the tray and then spray the adhesive on the front side.

4. Spread your fabric/paper smoothly onto the spray adhesive and pull tightly over the edge and stick it to the foam tape. Use more tape or glue to tidy and stick the corners.

5. Use the nail and hammer to carefully punch a hole through the top of the tray and thread through the cord to hang. Attach your photos, notes, and other items with the magnets.

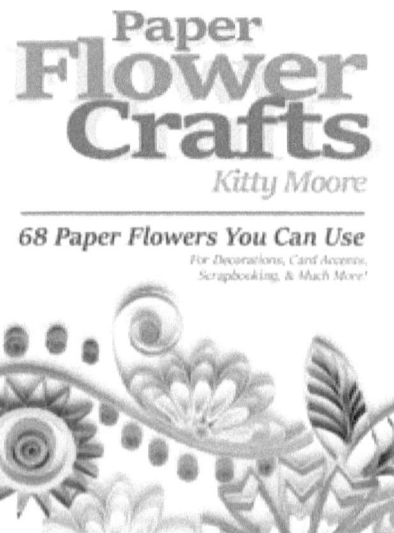

Check out Kitty's books at:

ArtsCraftsAndMore.com/go/books

16. A 'Grate' Earring Holder

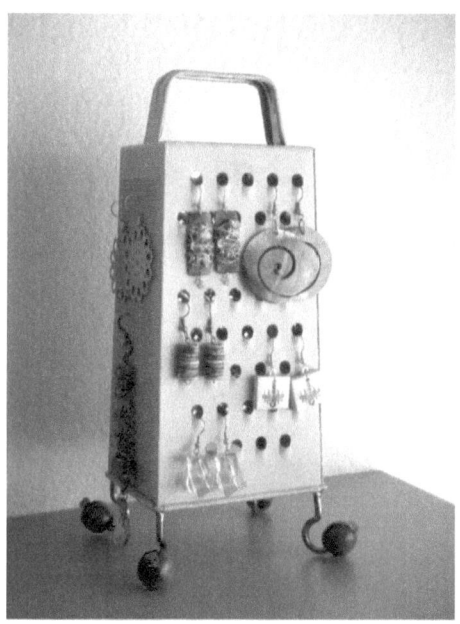

Materials

- Cheese grater
- Spray paint

Instructions

1. Make sure your grater is clean!
2. Use spray paint to get the perfect color and apply several thin coats to get the perfect finish. The grater's holes and hooks are perfect for hanging your earrings on.

17. Recycled T-Shirt Doormat

Materials

- 5-10 old t-shirts
- Scissors
- Hot glue gun and hot glue
- Doormat

Instructions

1. Cut the t-shirts into 2-inch strips, starting at the bottom. Cut each strip into 5-inch long strips.

2. Tie a knot in the middle of each strip (it will look like a bow). Make sure you have knotted every strip and ensured you have enough to cover the mat by spreading them over it.

3. Clear the mat and then place a line of hot glue along one side of the flat mat.

4. Stick each knot into the glue and press down, leaving about 1/4 inch between each one.

5. Complete the line and then glue another line about 1-inch from the first and repeat the process until the mat is covered. Finished! Just decide where your new rug will look and work best!

18. Always Open Hanging Laundry Bag

Materials

- Large pillowcase

- Embroidery hoop

- Fabric glue

- Cord

- Hook for back of the door

Instructions

1. Roll the top of the pillowcase around the embroidery hoop. Use fabric glue to create a seam to hold it in place.

2. Pierce a hole through the pillowcase and thread though the cord to create a loop before fixing it with a knot.

3. Fix the hook onto the back of the door and attach your new hanging, always-open laundry basket.

19. Gold Brick Bookends with Lace Trim

Materials

- 2 bricks
- Spray paint
- Lace fabric
- Glue
- Self-stick rubber pads

Instructions

1. Wash and clean the bricks thoroughly and be sure to remove all the dust. When they are dry wrap the lace

strip around the brick, measure and cut. Take the dry brick and cover it with white paint.

2. It will dry quite quickly and once it has, apply some glue to the lace strip and wrap it around the brick. The lace will act as a stencil, the white paint as an undercoat.

3. Carefully spray a coat of gold paint over the brick. Allow to dry and apply a second or more if necessary.

4. When it has dried delicately peel away the lace strip and reveal the white trim pattern. Now simply place the self-stick rubber pads at the bottom of the brick.

20. Box Tidy Chargers

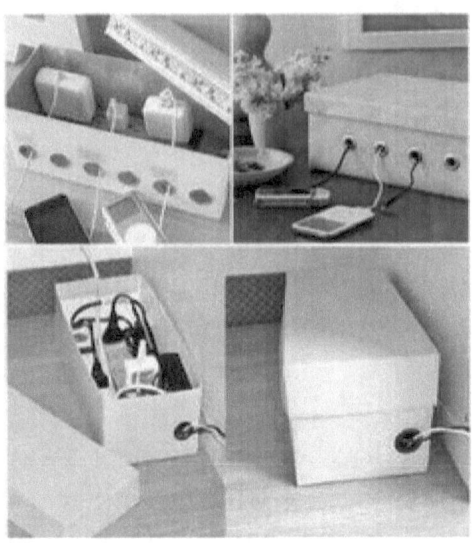

Materials

- Shoe box
- Paint and brush
- Craft knife
- Power extension cable

Instructions

1. You can use an old (but strong) shoe box and paint it whatever color you wish. Or spend some money on a small storage box. Make sure it's long enough to hold the extension cable and four power outlets.

2. When you have selected (and painted) your box, use your craft knife to cut a hole in the corner to allow the cable to feed through.

3. Mark out and carefully cut some small holes in the side of the box, think about how many you will need.

4. Plug in your chargers and pass the cords out through the holes. You can glue labels on the holes to identify what cable is for what device.

21. Colorful Cork Mobiles

Materials

- Corks from wine bottles
- Paint and brush
- Cocktail sticks
- Fishing line or cord to hang
- Small saw or cutting knife
- Wire clothes hanger

Instructions

1. Gather your corks and cut them into chunky discs. Paint the cork discs using the cocktail sticks to help

you hold them, pierce the stick through the cork and you should have be able to paint several on one stick.

2. When the cork discs have dried thread the fishing line, wire, or other cord through the holes and leave enough length for hanging.

3. Use the wire clothes hanger to make a support for the painted discs and tie them to it neatly. Decide where you want to hang it and secure it in place.

22. Clothesline Picture Gallery

Materials

- Photos
- Clothesline pins/pegs
- Cord
- Hammer and nails

Instructions

1. First you need a wall space that needs some brightening up. Next you need the photos that you want to hang.

2. Then simply bang a few nails in at either end of the wall and tie the cord around each, knotting securely at both ends and making sure it won't snag and

droop too much. Do the top one first and be sure you leave the right amount of space between the lines.

3. Use the clothes pins/pegs to hang your photos. Change the photos often to keep your gallery fresh. You're not restricted to only photos - hang tickets, cards, reminders and any other paper mementos you wish.

23. Old Belts Become Easy Shelving

Materials

- 2 wooden boards (approx 5"x1"x30")
- 4 long leather belts (more for longer shelves)
- Measuring tape and pencil
- Hammer
- Carpet tacks/short nails
- Long nails or screws and wall plugs (need drill)
- Spirit level (for hanging)

Instructions

1. Prepare your boards before starting - sand, fill any holes, paint or varnish if necessary, and allow to dry. Draw a straight line 2" from both ends of the board, on the back and front.

2. Fasten the belts and create two identical loops - there needs to be about a 60" circumference so you may need to attach two belts together. This might also require an extra hole being made in the belt - easily done using a drill, awl, or a hammer and nail.

3. Put the first board inside both belt loops and position them on the 2" lines you drew earlier. Think about where you want the belt buckles to be seen and avoid having them in line with the second shelf (ie. not 10" from the bottom).

4. When you have them in position, turn the board and belts over and hammer three carpet tacks into the belt to hold them in line. Repeat on the opposite side. Flip the boards onto their sides and hammer a nail into the front of each belt to give it greater strength and sturdiness.

5. With the board still on its side, measure 10" up and insert the second board on its side and hammer a nail through the center of the belt into the side of the board. Measure carefully and repeat for the other side to make sure your shelves will be level.

6. Double check the measurements before flipping your shelving unit over and hammering nails through the center of the belts on the reverse side. Lift the shelves and pull the loops tight to check that their lengths are identical. If you need to adjust them, simply make a new hole in the belt and resize using the buckle.

7. Use your spirit level when you are hanging them. You may require some assistance to hold them in place, and use longer nails to hammer through the belts at the top of the loop to fix them to your wall. Using screws with wall plugs will provide a more secure fixing. (Hammer or screw inside the top of the loop as the front will then hide the nail head from view.)

24. Bedroom to Boudoir

Materials

- Embroidery hoop (24" diameter)
- Command hook (for hanging)
- Two curtain panels
- Trim for the curtains
- Fabric glue
- Scissors

Instructions

1. Choose the fabric you want to have hanging over your bed, and embellish it by adding a decorative trim to its edge.

2. Position your curtain trim at the top of the curtain panel and run it down the length of the side, trimming it to size - use pins or tape to hold the trim in place and leave a space to enable you to squeeze out a line of fabric glue to attach the trim to the curtain. Keep the cut offs as you will need them soon.

3. Repeat the process for the other curtain panel and make sure you attach the trim on the opposite edge so that they are facing each other when hung.

4. Now you are ready to slide the curtains onto the embroidery hoop - make sure the good sides are facing out and if you have trimmed them start with those sides first. That way, when you hang them, the fittings that close the hoop will not be as visible.

5. After closing the loop, pierce the top of the curtains carefully to avoid tearing with the scissors. Make three equally spaced holes that are just big enough to thread through lengths of trim (or ribbon if preferred). Knot the ends of each to create three loops. Secure the command hook on the ceiling above your bed, gather the three loops, and hang your romantic bed canopy. Sweet dreams!

25. Kitchen Cool

Materials

- Vinyl or electrician's colored tape
- Ruler or measuring tape
- Craft knife and scissors

Instructions

1. This project is all about experimenting until you find the perfect colors and designs for your washing machine, refrigerator, cupboards, and other kitchen furniture. It's brilliant because the tape is easily removed without any damage meaning mistakes are

easily fixed - the designs are non-permanent so it's perfect for renters too. Once you start, the difficulty will be deciding where to stop!

2. Having chosen the tape, colors and design simply start sticking it to your dishwasher, cupboard doors, or wherever you want. Use the ruler to make sure your lines are parallel.

3. To get the perfect finish, trim the tape a little longer at both ends before using the craft knife to slice it precisely, taking care not to damage the surface underneath. It works in the bathroom, bedroom and living room too!

26. Fresh Air Door Stops

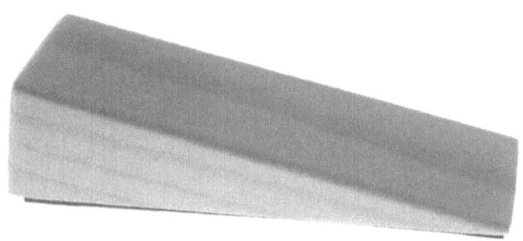

Materials

- 4"x4" block of wood (find them at your hardware store in the off-cuts section)

- Handsaw or chop saw

- Ruler and pencil

- Protractor for measuring angle

- Sandpaper

- Paint or varnish and brush

- Hot glue and gun

Instructions

1. The perfect doorstop is angled at 15 degrees. Use your protractor to measure the angle from one

corner and then draw a line with the ruler from the corner to the edge.

2. Be very careful when you cut along this line. If using the handsaw start on the long edge and cut towards the corner.

3. 2-for-1 BONUS!! Notice the off-cut - don't throw it away. You have the perfect angle to make another doorstop by simply drawing a straight line from the sharp end and cutting across it.

4. Smooth all the edges with the sand paper and paint or varnish the doorstops however you wish using any designs or combination of colors.

5. When dry flip the doorstop over and using the glue gun, apply three lines from side to side. When dry, these lines provide the anti-slip grip to keep the doorstops in place, as well as providing protection from scratches to the floor.

27. Super Shelves for Your Bathroom

Materials

- 3 equal lengths of wood (two 1"x4" lengths and one 1"x"2)

- 2" nails and hammer

- Sand paper

- Primer paint and filler

- Gloss paint and brushes

- Drill and screws

Instructions

1. Prepare the wood, sanding and smoothing any rough pieces and filling any holes.

2. Using the two 1"x4" lengths of wood, make an L-shape and nail the pieces together.

3. Now nail the 1"x2" length on one edge of the wood to create a lip for the shelf that will prevent the items that will go it from slipping off. Make sure you use enough nails and hammer them home to make the fixing secure.

4. Use filler to cover the nail holes and sand down. Prime the wood and allow to dry before painting with the gloss paint.

5. Drill pilot holes through the back length to make it easier to screw your new shelf to the wall.

28. Stunningly Simple Sofa Table

Materials

- 2 long boards either 1"x10" or 1"x12" (the dimensions are up to you)

- 2 1"x6" planks

- 2 brackets

- Handsaw

- 2" nails and hammer

- Sand paper

- Wood glue

- Paint or varnish and brushes

- Drill and screws

Instructions

1. Start by cutting your long boards to size, you need a top and two legs, measure up with your sofa to get the perfect size.

2. Now screw your bracket into the legs, making sure it is flush with the edge of the wood.

3. Next screw the top to the legs using the bracket and making sure the edges are flush.

4. Nail the 1"x2" length on one edge of the wood to create a lip for shelf, that will prevent the items that will go on it from slipping off.

5. To give your table strength you need to use the 1"x6" planks. Lie your table on its side and place the plank so that it runs diagonally from corner to corner. Mark a line where the edges overlap.

6. Cut this line with the saw and sand the edges. Check it is the correct length and flush with the legs before adding some wood glue and nailing into place.

7. Flip the table onto the other side and repeat the process, creating an X design with the planks. All you have to do now is decide whether to paint, stain, or varnish your brand-new sofa table.

29. Dress Your Sink to Beautify Your Bathroom

Materials

- Fabric (measure your sink's dimension and height from the floor)

- Scissors

- Ruler or measuring tape

- Fabric glue

- Hook-and-loop (Velcro) tape

- Paint or varnish and brushes

- Drill and screws

Instructions

1. Choose your fabric, a shower curtain is a cheap and effective fabric to use.

2. Measure your sink and cut the fabric to size. For easy access to the space under the sink, cut two pieces to create a curtain effect. Leave a few inches around the edges to create hems. Fold, iron and use the fabric glue to hold the hems in place.

3. Take the hook-and-loop tape and attach a strip around the base of the sink.

4. Attach the other side of the hook-and-loop tape to the top of each piece of fabric using the glue.

5. Attach the two pieces to the sink and say bid farewell to the unsightly pipes and plumbing!

30. 5 Minute Bathroom Storage Solution

Materials

- Wicker baskets (various sizes)
- Spirit level
- Drill, long screws, and wall plugs

Instructions

1. Measure your space and buy some sturdy, lightweight wicker baskets that would accommodate the size of your space. Two or three small ones will work and look better than one big one.

2. Decide where you want them and use your spirit level to make sure they are straight.

3. Drill four holes into the corners of each basket and use a pencil to mark the space on the wall.

4. Drill the wall and insert wall plugs for the screws.

5. Fix your baskets to the wall using the long screws and remember not to screw them fully in, leaving enough out to hold the basket securely to the wall. Use your new space to store all your bathroom towels or other items.

31. Trendy Yarn Lampshade

Materials

- Yarn
- Old lampshade
- Baking paper
- Tape
- Wallpaper adhesive
- Scissors
- Superglue

Instructions

1. Remove the central fixings from the existing lampshade and put to the side (you will need it for your new lampshade).

2. Cover the shade with baking paper, using tape to hold it in place. This makes sure the yarn won't stick to the shade.

3. Tape the first piece of yarn to the baking paper and then start whirling the yarn around the shade, creating your design - leave some gaps to get the trendy modern look.

4. When you have covered the shade cut the yarn and use tape to hold it in place.

5. Mix the wallpaper paste and gently dab it all over the yarn, making sure you have covered every piece.

6. Let the yarn dry. This can take a long time, perhaps even a couple of days, but you have to be patient.

7. Once dry, gently separate the yarn and baking paper. Use the superglue to attach the central fixings from your old shade so that you can reattach it to the lamp.

Conclusion

Now you see how quick and easy you can refresh your living space at minimal expense, why not experiment and adopt some of the 31 crafts detailed above by using different materials or combining techniques and ideas to come up with your own DIY crafts?

Last Chance to Get YOUR Bonus!

FOR A LIMITED TIME ONLY – Get my best-selling book "DIY Crafts: The 100 Most Popular Crafts & Projects That Make Your Life Easier" absolutely FREE!

Readers who have downloaded the bonus book as well have seen the greatest changes in their crafting abilities and have expanded their repertoire of crafts – so it is *highly recommended* to get this bonus book today!

Get your free copy at:

ArtsCraftsAndMore.com/Bonus

Final Words

Thank you for downloading this book!

I really hope that you have been inspired to create your own projects and that you will have a lot of fun crafting.

I do hope that you and your family have found lots of ways to fill lazy afternoons or rainy days in a more fun way.

If you have enjoyed this book and would like to share your positive thoughts, could you please take 30 seconds of your time to go back and give me a review on my Amazon book page!

I really appreciate these reviews because I like to know what people have thought about the book.

Again, thank you and have fun crafting!

Disclaimer

No Warranties: The authors and publishers don't guarantee or warrant the quality, accuracy, completeness, timeliness, appropriateness or suitability of the information in this book, or of any product or services referenced by this site.

The information in this site is provided on an "as is" basis and the authors and publishers make no representations or warranties of any kind with respect to this information. This site may contain inaccuracies, typographical errors, or other errors.

Liability Disclaimer: The publishers, authors, and other parties involved in the creation, production, provision of information, or delivery of this site specifically disclaim any responsibility, and shall not be held liable for any damages, claims, injuries, losses, liabilities, costs, or obligations including any direct, indirect, special, incidental, or consequences damages (collectively known as "Damages") whatsoever and howsoever caused, arising out of, or in connection with the use or misuse of the site and the information contained within it, whether such Damages arise in contract, tort, negligence, equity, statute law, or by way of other legal theory.

www.ingramcontent.com/pod-product-compliance
Lightning Source LLC
Chambersburg PA
CBHW021131080526
44587CB00012B/1237